Max is not a puppy anymore.

He is now as big as he will ever be.

He is white all over, with two dark brown eyes, a black nose, and droopy ears that flop up and down when he walks. He has a white tail that is always pointing up.

Max is not a big dog. He is bigger than a big cat, but smaller than many of the other dogs that he meets on the street.

He does not mind not being the biggest or strongest of all the dogs in the world. He is happy being the size that he is.

Max has been a member of our family almost all of his life.

When we first saw him at the pet store he was still a puppy, and we liked him so much we decided to bring him home with us.

He never had any other family.

Max depends on us and we always take good care of him: We feed him, make sure he has water to drink, wash him when he is dirty, and pet him very often.

Max is a brave dog. He is not afraid of bigger and stronger dogs, because he trusts that they will not hurt him.

Most of the time when he meets another dog on the street they sniff each other, saying "hello" in their own way, and sometimes even play together for a while.

You see, Max is blind. He cannot see at all. He cannot see what is in front of him, and if there is something in his way he does not know that.

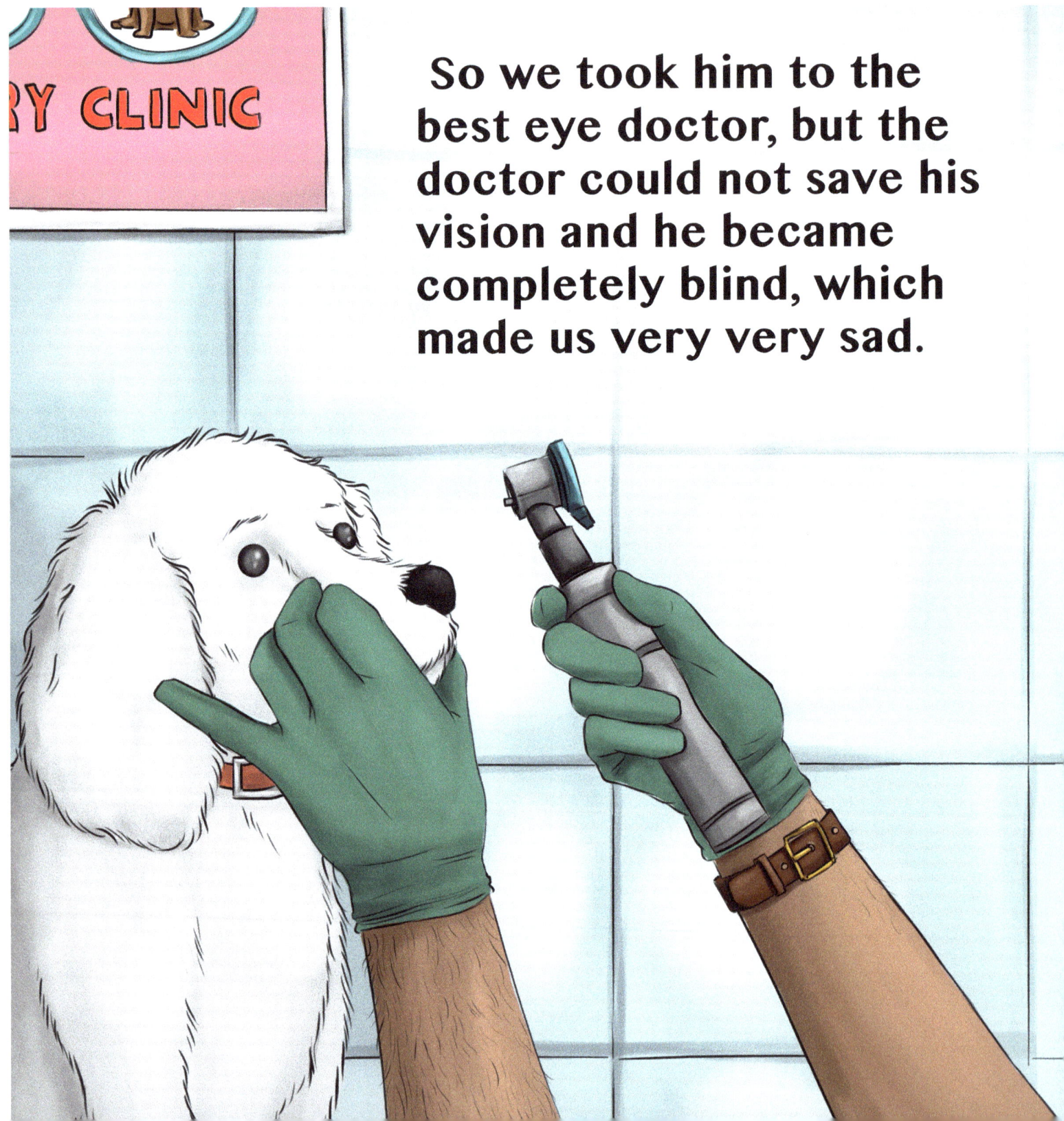

So we took him to the best eye doctor, but the doctor could not save his vision and he became completely blind, which made us very very sad.

And when he is about to bump into something, we can not tell him "watch out!" – Max is also deaf. Over time his hearing has gone away, and even if we shouted he could not hear us. He cannot hear a car coming down the street.

So we are his eyes and ears. We never let him off the leash, and protect him to not get hurt. While we are with him, no harm will come to our little dog Max.

Max is a really smart dog. He does not do tricks, but we are certain that he can count.

How do we know that?

We give him one of biscuit and he goes away to eat it.

When he comes back for another one we give him the second treat, and he goes away to eat it.

When he comes back for another one we give him the third treat, and he goes away to eat it.

In the beginning, Max would come back asking for another biscuit, and we would say "No more" and would not give him any more biscuits. So, after a while, Max learned that after the third biscuit he will not get another one, so he stopped coming to ask for it.

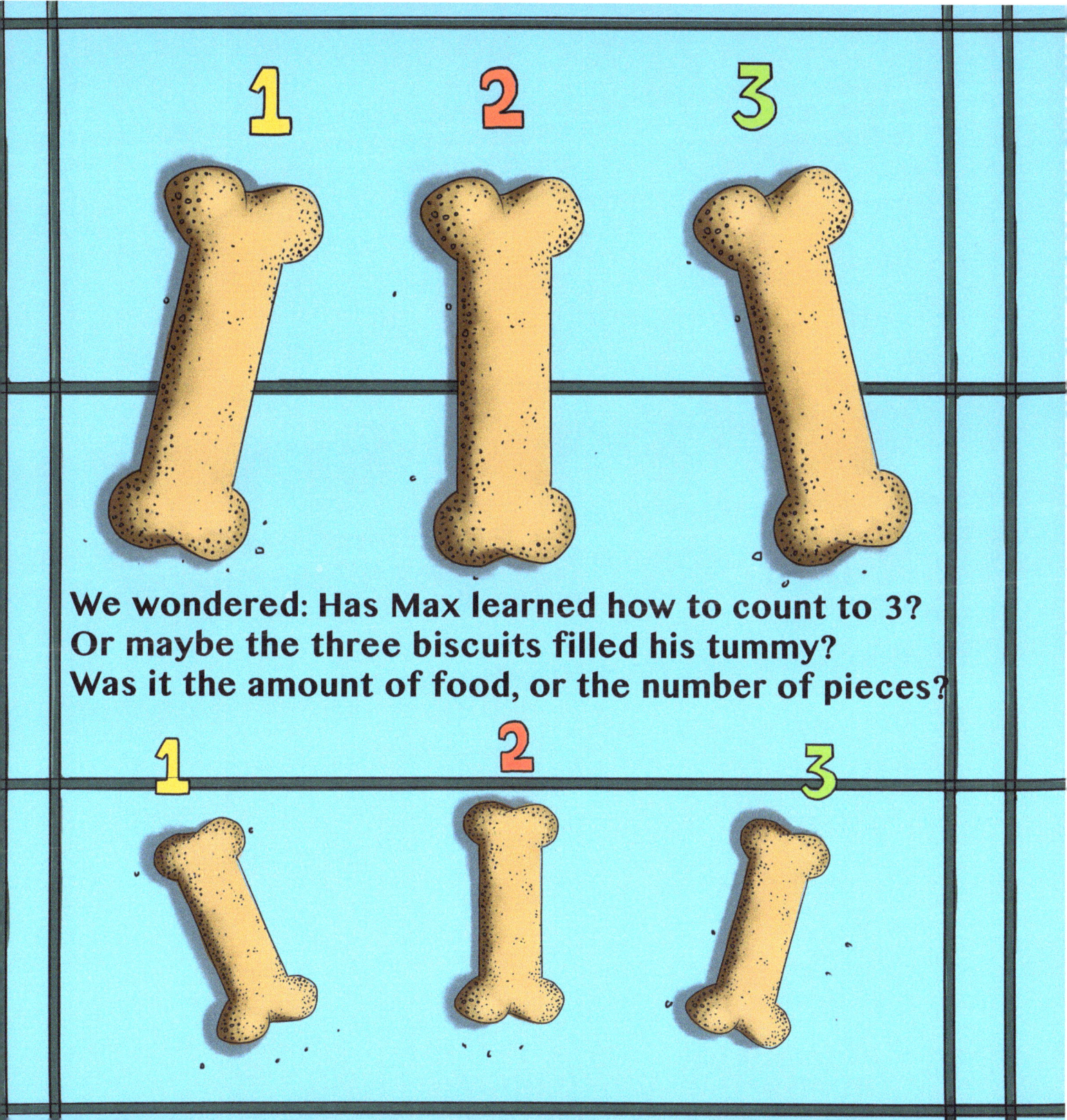

We wondered: Has Max learned how to count to 3?
Or maybe the three biscuits filled his tummy?
Was it the amount of food, or the number of pieces?

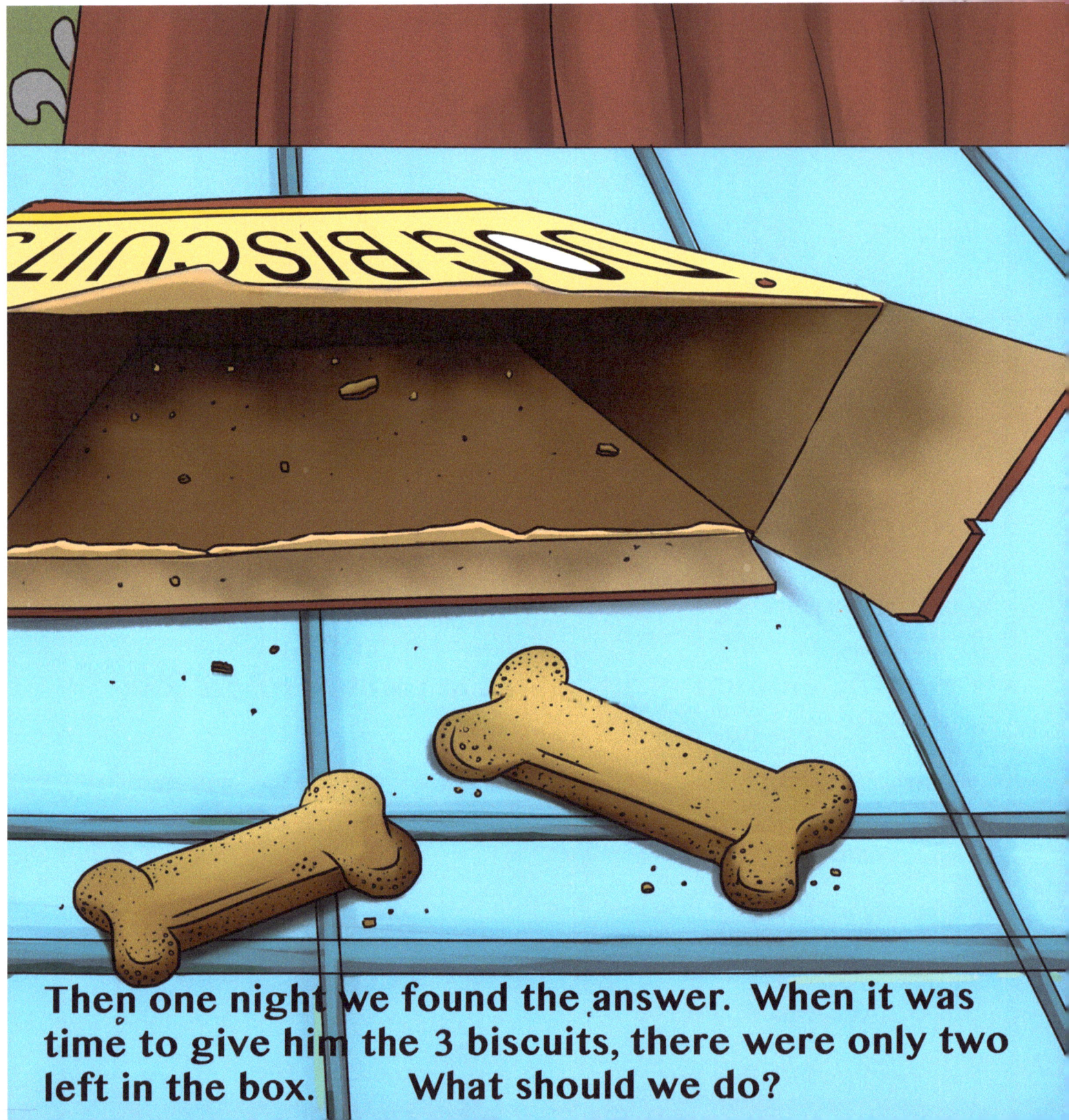
Then one night we found the answer. When it was time to give him the 3 biscuits, there were only two left in the box. What should we do?

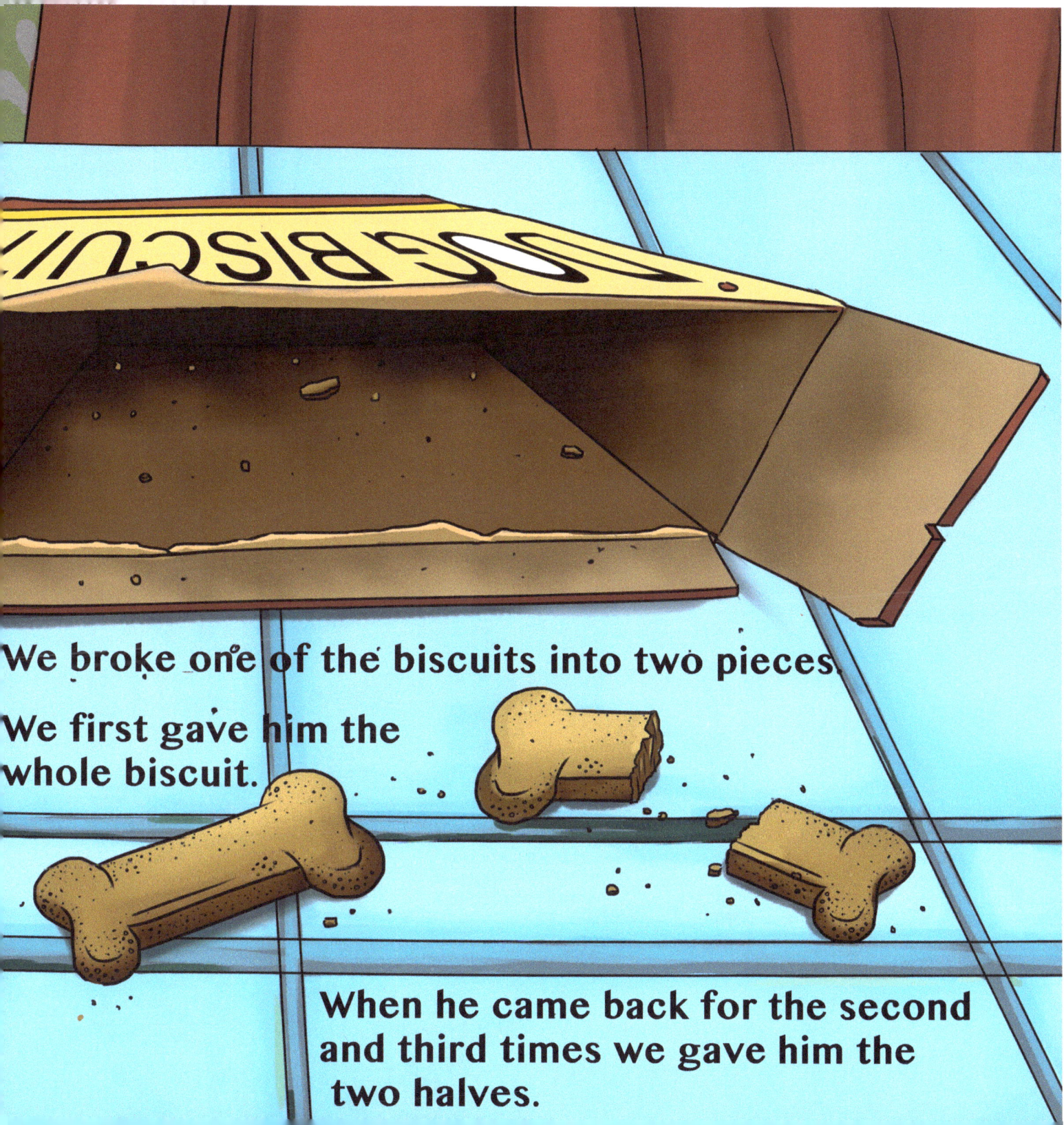

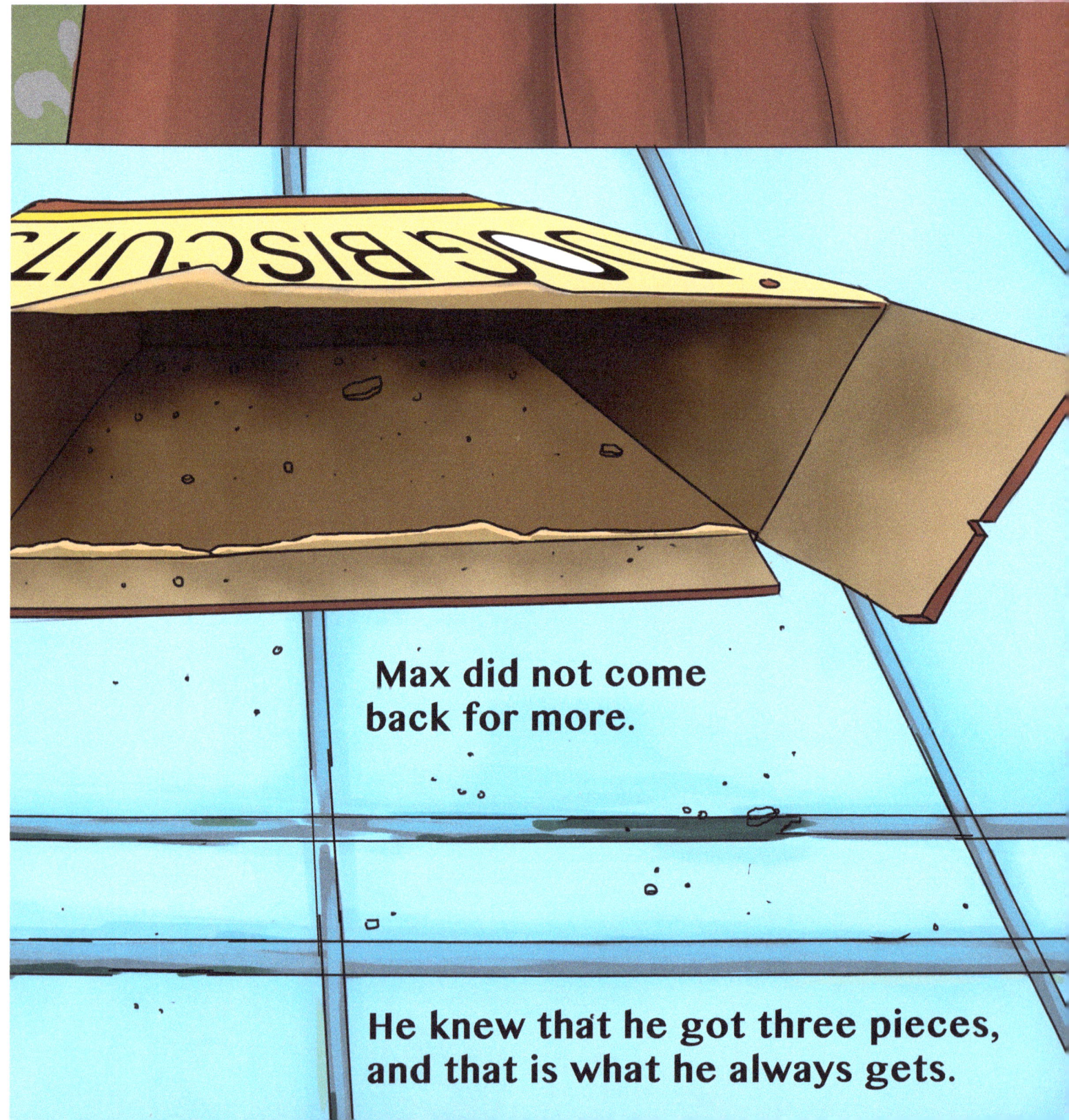

To make sure, the next night we broke one biscuit into three pieces, and sure enough, after the third piece he went to sleep happily.

Now we were certain:
Max can count to three!

Later we discovered just how smart Max really is:

Max can even count to seven!

How did we find that out?

<= 6   7 =>

Well, from our house there are two sets of stairs going to the street.

On one side there are **six** steps, on the other **seven**.

When we take Max out for his walk, we always come out of the house going down the seven steps.

In the beginning, after he became blind, Max would hesitate, lower his head and sniff the ground, checking to make sure if he needs to step down or walk forward. He would go:

> One...
> Two...
> Three...
> Four...
> Five...
> Six...
> Seven...

Then straighten out and walk on the sidewalk.

After a few days, he no longer needed to lower his head and sniff the ground.

He would trot down the steps:

one, two, three, four, five, six, and seven.

Max was counting the steps, all the way to seven.

On the way back, we would come through the other staircase, with only six steps. Here too, in the first few days Max would hesitate, climbing the steps slowly, one at a time:

> One...
> Two...
> Three...
> Four...
> Five...
> Six...

And then he would lift his front paw to climb the seventh step, but there was no seventh step.

After a few days he learned that there were only six steps going up, and he no longer was looking for the seventh.

Max is a very smart dog, and can count!

When we go to sleep at night, Max used to jump up on the bed, curl up by us like a big fluffy ball, always snuggling close to one of us. He would go to sleep knowing that we are near him.

Now that he is older, he cannot jump up on the bed anymore. He sits by the bed and cries and whimpers until we pick him up and bring him onto the bed.

Then he is happy again, and curls himself into a ball, and peacefully goes to sleep.

Max is a wonderful dog

www.ingramcontent.com/pod-product-compliance
Lightning Source LLC
LaVergne TN
LVHW072115060526
838200LV00061B/4896